Shaer -e- Win

Children's Book of Poems

Rhea Sajnani
Debbiejo Miranda

PARTRIDGE

To order additional copies of this book, contact
Toll Free 800 101 2657 (Singapore)
Toll Free 1 800 81 7340 (Malaysia)
orders.singapore@partridgepublishing.com

www.partridgepublishing.com/singapore

Contents

YET

I can't do this ... I am bad at it,
THINK about what you say...
Does it help you in anyway?
Or simply negates and hurts you.
Embrace struggles and challenges in your life, and
Remember that mistakes are the stepping-stones to
success,
Spread happiness and positivity all around you,
And strongly believe in If I can't do it Yet, I just need to
Try Try Try and then I Can Can Can!
Incorporate "I Can" in your life and see where it leads
A change of words will bring out the best within you
WIN believes in positivity and we believe in WIN,
Together WE can ...together WE will!

Lubna Naveed

"The mind is everything, what you think you achieve and become."

Andy the Lion

Abishek Kumar

I am supposed to use figurative language
And make a poem all by myself
I wish I can simply borrow one
From a book off the shelf.

Sometimes it's so simple
To simply sing a song
But perhaps it's not possible
To pen a poem.

My mind wonders like a wild goose, in the Wild West
I better get started and put all other thoughts to rest.

My poem's about a lion
Who was as strong as iron
But he also was as sweet as candy
His name was Andy.

He ran across the lush green fields, zoom...zoom
And chased a deer to its doom.

The deer was tired....
The lion perspired......

The deer pleaded "Please... let me go,
I have a family just like you"
Andy the lion replied, "Ok my deer
But this favour is due"

Andy was proud of his deed, he was happy in his heart
But he longed for meal... a – la –carte.

Hope you like this poem,
It's fickle but its new, I enjoyed writing it
Hope you like it too.

Food Chain

Hey! You green grasshoppers!
Beware of the mighty mice
Running between the files like a wheel

Hey! You squeaky mouse!
Beware of the slithery snake
Going Hiss! Hiss! All day long
You never know where you might go wrong!
Hey! You meandering snake!
The hawk is on the run
Hold your horses, you are the king of them all!
But alas! You have to meet your fate
Unto the earth you return
But it's never too late!
The decomposers are dancing towards your arrival
They work day and night
They create the magic of nutrients
And the circle of life continues...
As magnanimous miners for the plants...

Glazy Winter

Charissa De Silva

It was on a cold winter night
When the stars were shining so bright
The wolf was howling while the wind was blowing
The owl was as still as the moon
The lake wondered in its own pool

It's a glazy shade of winter
It's a glazy shade of winter
Awoooo!!!...... Howled the wolf
It's a glazy shade of winter
Ooo! Ooo! Ooo!
Said the owl in its own language
It's a glazy shade of winter

It's a glazy shade of winter
The wind whispered,
To the dead branches of the tree.
I know! I know! Said the trunk of the tree
It's the last week of........
CHRISTMAS

Halloween Night

Creepy crawlies in the night
If you want to survive you have to fight
Fell in the trap of a haunted house
Inside you'll find a shivering mouse
The haunted house as cold as ice
Giving you shivers down your spine
Thunder thunder booms shrick and shrack
They are coming there is no coming back
Gerry the ghost gleaming in the night
And he kills whoever comes in his sight
Open the gates with a little creak
Go inside and play hide and seek
The tower of doom swallows you
A drop of blood falls one or tow
Walk on the road with a whip cream
Wake up! Wake up! The dream screams

Faustine, kyla, Huzaifa

HaLLOWEEn FRiGHt

Raseel Khwaiss

It was a dark and stormy night
A nightmare with no escape in sight
It covered the land and sky in black,
But why?
It sulked through the abandoned street
On its heavy but silent feet
Like a vulture in the day
It removes all happiness in its way
A hiss of a cat running along
Singing its wretched screeching song
A mighty moon walking through the cloud
Hidden but found
Halloween, excitement and fear always seek
Thunder cracking sky
Birds abandon and fly

HOMEWORK

Asra Qureshi

I've told you once, I've told you twice
Forgetting homework just isn't nice
Homework is like getting dressed
Got to do it to be your best
You say it isn't fair,
But people do it everywhere.
Do it now, get it done.
I know, I know it isn't fun.
Homework is like cleaning your room,
Except you don't have to use a broom
Do it now, we'll give you a treat,
Something tasty and good to eat.

I LIKE Bananas

Dave Matthews

I like bananas
But I don't like piranhas
Bananas are yellow
And it's not white like marsh mellow
Bananas is my favourite fruit
Sometime I leave them in my Dad's suit
My friends think I am a monkey
But I think it's just funky.

LOOK OUTSIDE

Anisa Nurmatova

Look outside,
Can't you see?
The trees are crying and the flowers are dying.
The habitat of the Polar Bear is disappearing
as fast as melting ice it seems,
It's caused by all of us.
Things won't be like this in a year or two,
If pollution is all we do.
Every drop of water must be saved.
Industrial waste can be an intelligent
member of recycling movement.
The Earth is in a hazard, it can't help itself.
Show the World what you can do.

STOP POLLUTION!

THE DREAM WORLD OF YOURS

VADIM RIKUNOV

The dream world of yours
Will have all the colours of the rainbow, one at a time
With incredible brushes sketching over the world
Everything turning the true colour of light
Imagination is yours; straight short or even curled

The dream world of yours
Might have enormous snowflakes
falling down everyday
Or the raindrops the size of the football
It might even have sweltering
sunlight or ravenous storms
However, for sure, your weather would
always fascinate and enthral!

The dream world of yours
May have marvellous or terrific creatures,
From unicorns with horns as luminous as the sunrise
To the gruesome monster who wants you
slightly fried on an average heat
But all the same, it remains after you
whether to live with dragons or flies.

The dream world of yours
Might have futuristic, advanced technologies
Or old fashioned retro design
scattered all over the place
Humongous skyscrapers or
comfortable houses combined
In one single world, isn't that a grace?

The dream world of yours
Is where all the deep aspirations of yours come true
The little, marvellous wishes springing into life.
Everything floating as swift as though in thin air
The dream world is where everything goes
under the magic tune of your life

My Mother

JOEL JOSE

She rises like the sun
Buzzes like the bee
Makes yummy food
Sambhar, Sandwiches and spaghetti.

The house cheers up when she mops it clean.
The floor shines like a mirror.
With my face glaring at me.
She works hard and is so kind
But is sometimes mean, when out of her mind.

It happens when no one listens to her,
She gets so angry and Brrrr!!!!! It's scary.

Without her I won't be living,
God has given me peace and rest,
And also he gave me a mother
Who Is The Best!!!!!!!

THE FROG PRINCE

Julianna Ramanayuka

There once was a princess,
Who got a frog's interest?
This frog helped her by getting her ball
That's not all!!! No, that's not all

She make a promise to be his friend,
But that was never an attempt
The king said "Promises should always be kept!"
So the princess did accept

The frog was invited for lunch,
Played and they were a happy bunch
But when she saw him on her bed asleep
She threw him, which made him weep

Soon the princess realized her sins
And kissed him, which made him a prince
However, as he acted like a frog,
Had no choice but to keep him apart

The prince was heart broken
As the princess has not spoken
Soon he ran to the witch
In the hope of being a frog in a switch

THE HAUNTED HOUSE

Aaditya Gandhi

The haunted house stood at the stiff cliff
In all its eerie glory
The foggy mist, the glistening moonlight,
Foretold the dreaded fate of this scary spooky story

The door of the house creaked open
The windows slammed shut
A candle awakened in the distance
While the willows whispered tut, tut, tut

The wind howled
Bellowing in rage
Shouting in great fury
Feeling trapped in a humongous cage

The putrid stench
Of the six hissing snakes
Tattered cobwebs clinging to the corners,
But what are the stakes?

The creepy silence in the stillness of the house
Disrupted by the ticking of the clock
The darkness horrifying
Who gave that sudden mysterious knock?

Blinding battling bats flying away
In the hollow staircase maze
Suspicious sinful spiders shrieking away,
In a blink, in a daze.
A ghostly shadow lingers
It's the man without a face
He lives in the haunted house
Don't ever dare to enter this perilous place.

Two Little Cats

ANELA JENAMARI

Two playful fairy cats play in the dark
No dogs are in sight, not even a bark.

The stars are in the sky
Shining with their light.
Lights up the whole earth
With brightness in the night.

These two adorable playful cats
Are not afraid of anything
Not even bats.

Playing in the dark
Catching fireflies
"Zzzzz" says the firefly
Flying off he cries.

U.A.E THE LanD OF DREaMS

Janelle D'mello

The story starts like this,
On 2nd December 1971
6 Emirates signed to become one
In 1972 Ras Al Khaimah came
To be part of the U.A.E
Joining the game.

Everyone admires Burj Khalifa,
Watching over Dubai,
It's the tallest building in the world
It actually touches the sky!

There are 4 colours in the U.A.E flag
Red, white, black and green
U.A.E is a busy city
The busiest you might have seen!

From a desert area,
To a famous one
You might want to visit the beaches
And relax under the sun.

I hope you visit U.A.E
It's better than it seems
Because this is U.A.E
THE LAND OF DREAMS.

DEEP SEA DIVING

Janelle D'mello

As I listened to the water,
Bubbling and gushing,
I felt the water above my head,
Splashing and splushing.

The soft, whirling sound,
Of the wonderful sea.
Oh, how I love the splishing,
Of the sound right next to me.

Gurgle! Gurgle!
The noise of fish,
Swimming around,
This was my wish!

The splurting water,
What a lovely sound,
Of a beautiful dolphin,
Swimming around.

I love deep sea diving,
It's so much fun,
Playing with fish,
Away from the sun.

FOSSILS

- by Aishwarya Sundar

Fossils are prehistoric animals buried underground,
That are waiting for many years to be found
Mud and fossils bones,
Are years later transformed into stones

Archaeologists search for them,
But unfortunately not
Everyone is successful, in finding them

Cast fossil, Mold fossil, Trace fossil,
Transitional fossil and, True-Form fossil are,
The four different,
Main and, colossal fossils.
Primeval animal are very well preserved,
Are only experimented at and observed.
Primordial animals used to be alive,
But now has left us and therefore cannot be revived.

Fossils are not only interesting,
They are fascinating, spellbinding and thrilling.
You still might be thinking that fossils
are unexciting and boring,
No they're not, they are just truly amazing.

Fossils most of you think,
Might just be a log.
You would understand them,
If they had not hardened into a rock.

MY TEACHER
Ali Ahmed & Adam Khan

My teacher
Ms. Rhea

Rishit

My teacher is a good creature
That will help build my future
Without my teacher, I have no space
To help me make in this world a place
Our teacher makes us see
Who we will be
To make us smart, strong and make us learn
To see we have to earn
She gives us magic
That is not tragic
With the teacher our mind is clean
And shows us not to be mean

Nature

Mishal Faraz

The winds are blowing, the waters flowing.
Maybe a cloud is flying above the ground too.
Bells are ringing and the birds are singing

That's all nature for you
Storms in different forms might be a hindrance
And you feel reluctant to go out, I do too
But whether it's bad weather or not
That's all nature for you

Perfect Plants

HANA SOPHIA SHABAD

Give plants the factors
To make them grow,
If you do not do this,
The growing will slow.
Oxygen is the gas
That the leaves blow,
From the roots to the stems,
The water will flow,
And then to the leaves, it will go,
For the food the plant needs
The Sun to glow
An the temperature must be perfect
It cannot be low.

River, River!

CHENNELYN SAN PASWAL

The water flows down, from the source,
Kicking the water with force.
My body shivers whenever, I see rivers.
The floodplane are enormous, where the
airplane always land.
Ox-bow lake isn't fake.
Seeing a stream is my biggest dream.
Splish- splash as it flows, the water blows.

A river meets a tributary, and ends
up to be a estuary.
The boy hook the string, into the
spring to fetch a fish.
The river ends with a mouth without no doubt.

THE MAGIC OF SPRING

Asra Qureshi

Finally, the cold, harsh winter has passed,
And now comes Spring.
The newly hatched baby birds,
Will cause their mother to sing.

The warm sun comes out,
Baby blueberry blossoms are in bloom.
Beautiful roses will open up,
Smelling of sweet perfume.

Soft, morning winds,
Will flow through the tall trees.
There will be plenty of work,
For the busy honey bees.

From flower to flower,
As they fly & buzz all day.
Spring is that magical time,
During March, April and May.

All birds come out,
Tweeting and chirping.
Look at all the joy,
To the world that they bring.

Stand up once,
And go and see.
Take a deep breath,
Like the wind you'll feel.

"Wishh" and "wooshh",
The trees' leaves say.
And the trees, you'll see,
Literally dance in the day.

Happily, the children play and play,
And make a swing,
All this, and more,
Is the magic of Spring

THE EVER-CHANGING TIME

By Gokulan

Oh, how time flies, when you are having fun,
It seems like only a few minutes,
but hours have passed.
Oh, how time flies, when you are
playing an addicting game,
Can't wait to finish the next level,
shocked when you see the time.
But, unbelieving as it is, even time can change,
Oh, how time flies, when you are having fun,
It seems like only a few minutes,
but hours have passed.
No longer does it fly, now it's a moving snail.
When you are bored, doing nothing,
Waiting for the next lesson in school.
Oh, how time flies, when you are having fun,
It seems like only a few minutes,
but hours have passed.
Time will annoy you, lazing around,
Making 15 minutes to 15 hours.
The clock's hands slowly moving,
Relishing your anger and irritation.
Oh, how time flies, when you are having fun,
It seems like only a few minutes,
but hours have passed.

A Beautiful Sunset

DIVLEEN KAUR

ILLUSTRATOR: ZAIN ALA BEDEEN MATHKOOR

In front of me was a beautiful sunset,
A variety of different colours met.
Red, orange, yellow and blue,
And colours like pink and purple.
So bright was the scorching sun,
Slowly merging into the horizon.
The ocean was so peaceful and gleaming,
Just as all of it was seeming.
In the ocean, far away in sight,
There was an island bold and bright.
The wind was slowly breezing,
And the temperature was quite warming.
I gently sat on the smooth sand,
And picked up some of it with my hand.
It had some stones and pebbles and shells,
But also filled with interesting smells.
There were palm trees everywhere,
With some green grass here and there.
I was looking at the sunset before me,
And enjoying everything I see.

DEPTH

ALISHBA SHAHZAD
ILLUSTRATOR: AVIVA D'SOUZA

Beneath you lies the depth.
Some cry seeing you
Some sail through!

You see some tear apart
You see some with gigantic hearts!

Some say they need you
Yet some betray you!

Happily Dysfunctional

SHAYNE CARADANG

Look at me
From up above
Take care of me
And without a doubt
You'll keep me safe
I miss you
It's been too long
I'm sorry for everything
Everything I did wrong
Thank you for giving me
A chance
A chance to love
A chance to change
A chance to dream
And a chance to be
Happily Dysfunctional

MY FAMILY

ASHMEET KAUR

ILLUSTRATOR: SHARON REJI

A family is made of love and tears,
laughter and years.
It grows stronger with the passing of
time.
More precious with the making of memories.
Sometimes a family is made of ones
you don't like for a while...
but you love for a lifetime.
It's a gift whose value is found
not in numbers buts in its capacity
to love.

It's the place you find
someone to encourage you.
believe in you.
Celebrate with you and comfort you.

A family is where you heart
feels most at home because you're
always wanted, always welcomed
always needed, always loved.

Sonnet

SI CHEN LI

ILLUSTRATOR: ZAIN ALA BEDEEN MATHKOOR

Nature is one of our greatest teachers.
She isn't strict like any other.
She gives you the ultimate features.
Which some won't even bother.
Look deep into the gorgeous nature,
Then you will understand better.
She brightens your future,
And makes everything matter.
Nature is the art of god,
Take a walk in the forest.
And touch the smooth wood,
And be her kindest tourist.
The birds will change your mood,
Come on and show us you are the wildest.
Si-Chen Li

Sonnet 2

SI CHEN LI
ILLUSTRATOR: YOMNA FAKHRY

Sinchen Li- (limerik2)
The sun was replaced by night.
The sky became a beautiful sight.
It was no longer blue.
A purple colour it grew,
Then tiny stars appeared, shining so bright.

SPEED

JIHAN SAM THOMAS
ILLUSTRATOR: SHARON REJI

The key is turned, gas begins to burn
The pistons start to pump, the wheels begin to turn
The driver drops the clutch
The car needs that soft touch
The tires screech as the smoke appears
The driver gets his ultimate fear
The car speeds away like a fighter jet
The speed poses a huge threat
The corner comes up, the breaks get hit
The tires scream to find their grip
The brake rotors glow
To make the car slow
At the exit of the corner the car gets loose
The suspension takes heavy abuse
The cars exhaust is a lion's roar
The experience is anything but a bore

SUMMER EMBRACE

MAHTA MIRKABIRI
ILLUSTRATOR: PEGAH HAZARI

The sun showers his rays,
on my already sunburnt face,
and I welcome the sweet embrace.

The smell of salt in all my clothes,
the sand between my toes.

A deep breath as I relax,
while eating from my bag of snacks.

The wind gently pushes my hair back,
and I can see no more black.

SUMMER FILLED WITH GOLD

SHIVA SHAKERI
ILLUSTRATOR: PEGAH HAZARI

A flower of gold how sweet you are,
so colourful so vibrant as sweet as
honeycomb,
your eyes are as the golden rays
of the sun

Is it winter or is it spring,
who can tell, when there is a mist of love
that curves your beautiful hands,
now it is summer filled with life of gold,
only the heavens can understand what this
life of happiness
could unfold

It lights up like a candle, like a flower it blooms,
like pieces of gold pinned on stems in a meadow,
oh what a summer
filled with gold

THE BEACH...

GITHMI MANODYA SIRIWARDANA
ILLUSTRATOR: SHARON REJI

THE BEACH

The sun is shining adding more vibrance to the rich
blue sky,
as I watched the birds fly

"Swish" I run towards the water as the soft and wet
sand kisses the sole of my feet,
It made me forget about the heat

I can hear laughter everywhere,
not a single tear to be found anywhere
A beautiful picture is painted as the children play
and people say "what a day at the beach"

THE RUGBY MATCH

INGRID ALBERTS
ILLUSTRATOR: YOMNA FAKHRY

Last month I witnessed a live rugby match.
On my vacation this was the only thing my eye could catch.
The atmosphere was simply amazing.
It was really cold, so obviously the sun wasn't blazing.

Stadium packed with a variety,
So full you'd barely hear yourself.
Clammed up with so much anxiety.
Just lingering for the match to start.

South Africa proudly flares their white and gold,
And New Zealand their black and white.
Both teams seen so strong and bold.
Just look at their supporters gazing with delight.

Whilst singing their national anthem loudly,
The players stand tall and proudly.
As it ends, the match starts.
Each team fighting to gain top in the charts.

This was a truly magnificent site.
Even though South Africa had lost,
They appeared humble.
And that's what was right.

THE TIGER-LILLY

KARIMAH SUJAWAL
ILLUSTRATOR: SHAYNE CARADANG

Tiger-Lilly stands for wealth and prosperity
No wonder it grows in the colour yellow gold
How a divine beauty
Those flowers are intensively bold

Growing in my garden today
As we speak
Amongst the green as they sway
Especially at its peak

That set fragrant smell
So silky and soft
I could smell it from the bottom of a well
Such a treasure, I could hide it in my secret loft

It is a staggering creation
From him above
To almost every nation
Brought down, for us to shout it our love

THE URCHIN

TIANNA MENDONCA

ILLUSTRATOR: YOMNA FAKHRY

Using their whole body as a compound eye,
They use their clandestine mouth to pry,
Into all sorts of coral reef,
Drilling it brisk and brief

Lurching vaguely on the levelled ocean floor,
Like predators hunting for prey,
So elusive, no one can possess,
The long, black, poison tipped antennae mutely clacking,
The sweltering ambience kept them slacking,
And submerged underwater,
For the rest of the summer.

THE URGE TO FLY

MELISSA FROMINA
ILLUSTRATOR: NAKUL RAJIV

~ THE URGE TO FLY

Shrivelled snails tried to escape,
An attempt to start a new life
Is what iced their souls.

To escape the colourless ground,
Something they Vision every dawn and dusk,
A little bit of hope remains.

Though the road is long,
Hope guides each soul to a rather hopeless,
But attainable definition of freedom.

The forlorn urge to fly,
Is a feeling even the smallest creatures,
Can experience in utter despair.

TOWER BRIDGE

ESHA SHARMA
ILLUSTRATOR: AVIVA D'SOUZA

Towering, tall and tantalizing, the tower bridge stands
Over the massive boats bobbling in the
Water with waves
Engulfing fish and life
Roaring and rumbling.

Bewitching is its beauty
Ravishing like the crown jewels
In the heart of London it stands
Dazzling diamonds fail to surpass its glory; the
Grandeur it exudes shames all other
Eastside it stands.

A Midnight Wanderer

SIDRA RAHIMY

I was a midnight wanderer in a world full of terrors.
Terrors not of beasts and giant creatures.
But of men and their fleeting thoughts; of their
loaded words more potent than any poison.

I was a midnight wanderer in a world full of terrors.
Not anymore.
I live amongst the terror of men and their
fleeting thoughts; of their loaded words.
For when dawn breaks and terrors fade, the world of
men is full of dreams even though they lay awake.

– Sidra Rahimy

THE FREE SPIRITED FLYER

SIDRA RAHIMY

When I was young I would see angels.
But now I am old and all I see are demons.

When I was young I saw wonders.
But now I am old and all I see is a shambles.

When I was young I dared to be free.
But now I am old and I am caged as can be.

When I was young I had a mind of my own.
But now I am old and I have become
what others want me to be.

When I was young my soul was alive.
But now I am old and dead is my mind.

When I was young I was truly me.
But now I am old and I live in the shell of
someone I would have never wanted to be.

When I was young I could fly as
far as the eye could see.
But now I am old, because they took
my wings away from me.

A WORLD OF WISHES

I wish I could be young again; turn
back the gears of time if I can.

I wish I could have a mind unbound; free
of thoughts of fear that hound.

I wish I could be free of the darkness; to regain
all the strength that I had harnessed.

I wish I had eyes then to see, what
the world would make of me.

I wish I had not wished to be she or he;
now I have caused time to flee.

I wish I had not left it so late to agree, that the only
thing I should have ever wished for was to be me.

I stood witness the day you left the light.
People thought me crazy for I did
not weep nor put up a fight.

For people know not that I have seen glimpses
of you, and so I shall forevermore.

For people know not that we are yet to meet
again, this time in the valley of despair.
A trip lasting eternity, not a penny needed for fare.

For people know not that only death will
bring together that life gladly tore apart.
And it shall be soon, dear friend, when we
shall meet, of that I am sure in my heart.

For people know not that you now
reside in the land of the night.
Ruled over by souls who had once too been
tortured by men; now free of their fright.

Time?

BEVERLEE DÇRUZ

I am the watcher on the wall.
And the listener in the lane.

I am the shadow lurking around the corner.
And the predator awaiting her prey.

I am enlightenment to the soul.
Yet potent to the form.

I am become death.
And saviour all at once.

I am an illusion.
Yet seem ever so real.

I have seen the beginning.
And I will surely see The End.

But WE need more help

GIAN WALDO

The oceans bubble and foam, like acidic soap
With specks of dead fish and corals to scrub away the
oils.
The forests moan and fall, like popular furniture
Fast disappearing in the markets with a greener future.
The streams fill and clog, like gutters
Filled with scraps and thrash in an untended clutter.
The air is tight and pungent, like toxic aerosol
With nauseating odours that burn through the Earth's
soul.
The temperature rises and overflows, like a heated
cooking basin
Overflowing and boiling, threatening to melt the casing.
The weather comes and goes quickly, like prices
Of depleting resources and increasing consumer items.

Creatures great and small, thin and hungry
For what lays in a garbage bag: crunchy, chunky and
incredibly funky
Beasts roaming free, captive and dying
By plastic ties, boxes and chemicals from thrash slowly
expiring

Men naïve and ignorant, shocked and disgusted
When they find little pieces of plastic in fish they ingested
Men apathetic but able, consume and live wastefully
While the whole world trembles, decays and boils carefully.
Groups small yet committed, striving and lobbying
For factories and individuals to stop their pollutive dumping.
Individuals alone yet committed, changing and fighting
To protect animals, plants and environment fast-disappearing.
Slowly but surely, we'll have a greener future to look after –
Bright and clean, where we can hear the rustle of leaves and joyful laughter.

Could've Been But Never Were

NEHAA TARIQ

Your lips curve into a smile
and my heart stutters
my ribs close around it
whispering

wait for it
wait for it
wait for it

your eyes crinkle with laughter
and my heart becomes a firework
wanting to shoot out my throat in the form of
oh god you're cute
oh god will you lay on dewy grass with me and tell me
your deepest secrets?
Oh god can we sit so entwined that I can't tell whose
heart beats so erratically?
Oh god oh god oh god
we could be so great
you and me
we could have been great.

Your laughter dies down but the fire in my chest doesn't.
I could have swallowed ice cubes whole but that fire
wouldn't die.

Who likes to play with fire?
Not you, for sure
so I gulp down water and bite my tongue
I feel my ribs contract and expand
every bated breath a whisper of
we could have been but we won't be
I'd sooner let myself wither then burn you with my
toxic fire
so I swallow my heart like a bitter pill
and wait for my lungs to sob it a lullaby
you can't have this one
you can't have this one
you can't have this one

And thus
I bury my heart
into a grave that's been filled and dug out too many
times,
the tombstone reading

The one that could've been.

Dead Doves and Burning Flags

GIAN WALDO

The streets hustle-bustle, people chitter-chatter
In pleasant, placid cafes, naïve laughter
Under the ever-shining sunlight; opulence glitters
In jewellery, smiles, water and wheat; loud, cacophonic
banter
In the busy markets, booming suddenly after
Grey boxes cut friendly laughter, spurting thick, dark
burgundy in the gutter.

It struck the white dove that flew,
Which grew weak with a serpent's violent breath,
And intoxicating Aries with enmity, hatred and greed
From the corrupt and spiteful's wicked brew,
Leading Aries by his horned head
To trample opulent nations and defiant enemies.

Caught in between people cry out, but the scales are
rusty;
Serpents, wolves, elephants and donkeys misuse it
While the innocent see patches of rotting ivory, long
pork and burgundy
Roses, adorning dead doves and burning flags on the grit
Of broken towns and burial grounds in the country
While the world waits for able leaders to commit.

In secluded wails, white poppies are laid
Near olive branches and sons that fell; in fractured dreams
Paper cranes glide pass a glade
Of explosive shells, while broken rifles flow downstream
When joy and laughter eventually returns
With transient peace like migratory birds.

Hence like the seasons, peace comes and goes
Along with vindictive, rapacious, patriotic reasons to spark woes.
But there will be a time, a time of joyous hosts
And singing in every mount and clime, relieved of their throes,
As eternal peace and unity returns, while of wicked hearts justice will dispose
And heavenly love, light, grace and repose
Will be disclosed and bestowed.

FRIENDSHIP

DINA NAEL

I must know, are you a true friend?
Will you stand by me until the end?
Neither of us is without any flaws
I will accept yours but will you accept mine?
I will be your shoulder to cry on when you're blue,
Will you be there for me when I am too?
I will take your hand and wipe your tears,
Will you hold me and soothe my fears?
I can bring joy and warm smiles,
Can we share that from a thousand miles?
Never will I forget what matters to you,
But will you remember what's vital to me too?
With you my cherished memories I'll share,
If only I was certain of how much you cared
But if you can accept me as I do you,
Then I am certain that you are a friend so true.

Justice is a Mythical Creature

JEWELLYN BARBOZA

Justice? What is 'justice'?
by definition – the principle of being fair; righteousness,
equitableness;
in reality – something that most people deserve, yet
often have to settle for less.

A cause people strive for, a cause people die for,
sometimes a cause other people decide to turn a blind
eye for.

'Justice is always served,' they say,
but that is not what the Syrians think as they walk over
the craters bombed into their roads,
and that is not what the four million refugees in camps
believe when they live in fear of returning home.

Is it right when a fifteen-year old girl is shot in the head?
The Nobel Peace prize would have never justified her
death.
She pushed for education - "books, not bullets."
Malala campaigned for equality, it is our duty to fulfill it.

'Justice is always served,' they say,
but Michael Brown was only eighteen, he didn't ask to die,
and "Hands up, don't shoot!" became an international cry.
Racial violence, systematic injustice –
'it's all in the past!'
Then why is #blacklivesmatter trending on social media?
And why are people of colour seen as a threat;
herded like sheep into a field, be quiet or it's death.

Yes, the world came together when Paris was attacked.
There was no racial division, no brown, white or black.
But religion was blamed, innocent people at stake.
An entire group held accountable for another's mistake.

We painted the world blue, red and white, a symbol of
support.
But does that ever bring back to life the irrecoverable
lives that were lost?

Justice - a cause people strive for, a cause people
die for,
sometimes a cause other people decide to turn a blind
eye for.

Mare Liberum

BEHSHID BEHROUZI

To set the world free,
You'd have to see;
What clasps its imprisonment,
So you cannot testify claiming 'lack of acknowledgement;'

Adolescents like you and me,
Forced to pay their country's greedy fee
Scattered around the world they are famished and droughty;
Imprisoned by robust chains of poverty

Take me to the see of freedom,
Where none is found of racism
Let me sail my boat proud,
Reinforced by a cheery crowd

Divide me not from rich or poor
There is no need for this extra chore
Favour them not for their pulchritude,
From these tasks take interlude

Then ye' will be taken to the see of freedom,
Where politics and wars are seldom
All aboard the ship of tranquility,
There you may rejoice for infinity.

Metal and Steel

JOSEPH BACANI

In this metal and steel metropolis,
The fullness of so-called success,
Inside the metal is a hollow shell of dull of intense
ferocity,
Waiting for the moment to wither and regress.

A pretentious and false image of life,
Where work and death walk in stride,
Often ending in pain and strife,
The adults have always hid and lied.

Do not fall prey to their bittersweet claims,
Once the routine has started, there is no ending.
There will only be you and none other to blame,
You've fallen to their social norm and shallow living.

They say that metal and steel make things stronger,
Why do you seem so weak and fragile?
Your eyes lack the luster of a dreamer
Only the dead pan eyes remain so vile.

In this ironic life of weak people and strong foundations,
Dreams are the haven of those yearning for one,
Reality is the realm of subtle dead creations,
Whether to drift between or stay in one is your decision to be done.

I am guilty of a dreaded sin that plagues my days,
My craven need for something more and everything beyond,
Nothing puts me at rest or lets my curiosity lay.
I, too, have been fighting this normality that I have donned.

Mother Earth

SIDRA RAHIMY

We call her mother yet treat her as a slave

We kill the rest of her children then
claim to be her favourite.

We poison her then wonder why
when she starts to choke.

We threaten her very being yet when she
tries to protect herself, we gasp and think;
could she possibly threaten her own?

We have bled her dry yet worry
about her pale complexion.

We cut off her arms yet wail
when she cannot feed us.

We turn a blind eye to her tears and
her warnings fall on deaf ears.

We call her mother, but we don't
deserve to be called her children.

Mother Nurture

AEVERIE POLINTAN

My mother would be an elephant
And I, her calf, born blind from the world
Clueless and naïve
A full time baby sitter
An 'all mother' she is

My mother would be an alligator
And I, her hatchling
Cold blooded she may seem
Threaten me and you shall see
How fierce and feisty she really is

My mother would be a cheetah
And I, her cub
Instincts I may not have
To give me sense is what she does
The greatest governess is who she is

My mother would be an orangutan
And I, her young
Comfort is what I seek
Denies she never does
Cuddles is what she gives

My mother would be an otter
And I, her whelp
Grounded and closed
Engulfed in her kelp,
she makes me feel safe

My mother would be a seal
And I, her pup
In the midst of thousands
She can see and spot
She knows me inside and out

My mother is a special woman
And I, her child
Tethered to life
Her love knows no bounds
To infinity and beyond

THE FACE OF TERRORISM

ALEENA ROSE

Shrieks vibrate through the ambience of the town
As dawn chooses to make an entrance
People scatter through to find security
Even though deep down they know it's an absolute
unavailability.
They muddle through the streets in darkness with
immense terror
Like pieces being moved on a chessboard by a higher
power

In the distant, yet another explosion transpire
Causing another hundred lives of mortals to expire
A child desperately holds on to his fallen mother
Shaking her with all his might pleading to God to pipe
away all the unpleasant matters

Lungs fill with smoke
While the hearts sink down in a choke
A pistol points at my torso
As air clears presenting the countenance of the
terrorist also

The masked man behind the gun pulls the trigger
My life ends quicker
Doing me a favor
As it all ends forever

Tranquility is all we ask for and all we need
But all we do cry and plead
Harmony would be a great deed
Let us all not just die and bleed.

THE LaCK OF UNITY

SANEAH SIDDIQUI

As the Earth spins on its axis
It is clearly evident how it has become fractious
With wars arising from every corner
Both men and women have been classed as mindless
mourners
Hence, countries board their walls up higher
Telling, yelling and crying for refugees to stop seeking
safety from them or they'll take aim and fire
Is this the world we want to live in?

Black, white, brown
Words that should not cause one to frown
Colours that should not be given more power
Yet here we are, seeing many people stay at home and
cower
In fear we are living of the judgement by others
Even though we were not raised that way by our
mothers
Is this the world we want to live in?

Women are being degraded
Whilst men's' status' upgraded
For things that should be refrained from being applauded
Seems to me these people are deluded
Respect is something we all deserve
Equally it should be preserved

Is this the world we want to live in?
Many people have been immersed in poverty
Why are we not making them our main priority?
Children's stomachs are rumbling with affliction
And then there is us, who have no restriction
With food, shelter, clothes and water
'AHHH' there's the scream of another woman who has
just lost her daughter
Is this the world we want to live in?

As our rambunctious fetish for technology can only be
described as greed
It comes to my attention that mankind is a dying breed
The omissions from these industries disintegrating
through the atmosphere
The one thing that is rarely regarded as another factor
for the damaged stratosphere
Must we need all of these technological advancements?
Our lives at stake as well as being the expense for all
of these enhancements
Is this the world we want to live in?

Harmony is all we need
In order to achieve as well as succeed
Working together hand in hand
Definitely will be our final stand
To fight injustice and all sin
That is the world we want to live in

THE STRENGTH OF HOPE

NIRANJANA RAMAKRISHNAN

Encased in a world enduring bloodshed,
A reign of carnage and desolation seems foreordained,
For as men propel their selves to the charms of the changing order,
The cries of those in despair are seldom seen without a shadowy air of disdain,

Yet the throb of aching hearts,
Their stories penned in blood and tears,
Dare to envision a future of a peaceful hearth,
On the coast of a buoyant new frontier,

Man scarcely seeks to fathom the strength of such belief,
For who amongst us can fathom the real strength of dreams?
Yet there remains a sense of strength in a perseverant mind,
Emboldened, defiant – refusing to tear at the seams,

The tales of those long gone show this to be true,
In the span of time, resilience and hope have been seldom shown defeat,
Like the treacherous journey that was embarked on by those fleeing war,
These acts of hope are lauded by us as many a remarkable feat,

Yet the throb of aching hearts,
Their stories penned in blood and tears,
Dare to envision a future of a peaceful hearth,
On the coast of a buoyant new frontier,

Such is the spirit that lies within a human heart,
Known to man by many-a name,
Strength, perseverance or resilience - or so it has been called,
Regardless of name, it is the strength of hope in these that remains the same.

Wнат ιѕ ιт?

ALETHEA BARRETO

What is it that passes through
the thick green canopy
invading the lush foliage of the upper boughs
to bring life to those underneath?

What is it that fills to brim
the eyes of the selfless mother
watching her child trained to be grim
in service of the nation and others?

What is it that binds one
human to another,
without a blood tie to demarcate
a relationship that can withstand trouble?

What is it that motivates
a child to grow into an adult
earning one's livelihood independently
and feeding several stomachs?

What is it that doesn't fail to
keep humanity in check when
incessant wars rage on and
mankind loses its depth?

Is it not hope,
the flittering ray of light enough to
break the clutches of darkness, the
gushing of tears of pride that depict
strength and fearlessness

Is it not hope,
the stronger-than-blood
unbreakable bond of courage,
the revitalizing will to go on and
live each day to the fullest

Is it not hope,
the only true ally of one and all,
the solution to blood-spilling battles
and Adam's fall.

TOGEtHER WE can

Together we can....
Sail through rough seas and storms,
Together we can....
move the mountains.
It takes effort and determination,
Unity strengthens ties.
Together we can...
nurture the minds of our children,
inculcate values and faith
and bring out the best in them.
Together we can ...and we always will.
As we believe that Every child matters

Lubna Naveed
Form Tutor Year 1 B

Printed in the United States
By Bookmasters